SMALL FIRES

T0158442

THE HUGH MACLENNAN POETRY SERIES

Editors: Allan Hepburn and Carolyn Smart

TITLES IN THE SERIES

Small Fires

Kelly Norah Drukker

McGill-Queen's University Press
Montreal & Kingston • London • Chicago

© Kelly Norah Drukker 2016

ISBN 978-0-7735-4770-4 (paper)
ISBN 978-0-7735-9948-2 (ePDF)
ISBN 978-0-7735-9949-9 (ePUB)

Legal deposit second quarter 2016
Bibliothèque nationale du Québec

Printed in Canada on acid-free paper that is 100% ancient forest free (100% post-consumer recycled), processed chlorine free

McGill-Queen's University Press acknowledges the support of the Canada Council for the Arts for our publishing program. We also acknowledge the financial support of the Government of Canada through the Canada Book Fund for our publishing activities.

Library and Archives Canada Cataloguing in Publication

Drukker, Kelly Norah, 1975–, author
  Small fires / Kelly Norah Drukker.

(Hugh MacLennan poetry series)
Issued in print and electronic formats.
ISBN 978-0-7735-4770-4 (paper). – ISBN 978-0-7735-9948-2 (ePDF). –
ISBN 978-0-7735-9949-9 (ePUB)

I. Title. II. Series: Hugh MacLennan poetry series

PS8607.R7475S63 2016   C811'.6   C2016-901771-0
                                                C2016-901772-9

This book was typeset by Interscript in 9.5/13 New Baskerville.

CONTENTS

I

V

THE BURNING HOUSE

I

On Inis Mór

*... what captivated me ... were the immensities in which
this little place is wrapped ... the processions of grey squalls
that stride in from the Atlantic's horizon ... the breakers
that continue to arch up, foam and fall across the shoals ...
the long, wind-rattled nights ...*
                    Tim Robinson, *Stones of Aran: Pilgrimage*

AT THE SEVEN CHURCHES
(NA SEACHT dTEAMPAILL)

Clochán, like a bell –
turned inward. Sound

of the wind in the fields.
No prayers, no mass, only

cows in the winter, making
their rounds. We come

to kneel at the doorway,
to peer into that kind of

dark. To think our way
backwards, listening.

~

East

━━━━━━━━━━━

THE FERRY IN

Driving through Rossaveal, all is stone and gnash. Scarred back of Connaught, stones where farmers wanted cabbages. Everything in its place and nothing where it should be. When they were swept here, by Cromwell's army, the people tumbled like stones from a barrow. Landed, haphazard, wherever they were and stayed. Landed unlike the gentry, who descended on wings made of sails, who nurtured roses in stone enclosures. Walls built to keep the people out. In Rossaveal, through the window of the Bus Éireann, you see how the stones seem to leap from the earth, but then stop, frozen, half-emerged, their feet still covered with moss.

We pass small white houses with leaning wooden barns, and beside them, older stone structures that could have been houses or small chapels. Maybe the people, fearing already for what little they had, did not tear them down but left them standing. Built homes and sheds around them, hung clotheslines, laundry drying in the breeze beside dead-eyed structures centuries old.

When the bus turns a corner and stops in the car park across from the harbour, the women at the back stand up, impatient. They are carrying bags made of canvas with straining zippers, filled with produce and goods from the mainland. Jumpers and raincoats and watches from Dunnes Stores; carrots in cellophane, bunches of grapes, sweet potatoes they would pay three times as much for on the island. As we step off the bus, there is talk and chatter as they carry their bags and wheel their suitcases to the pier where the ferry stands, waiting. Seagulls hurl shrill cries down to the men on deck eating crisps from bags and drinking coffee from Styrofoam cups. From the deck below, a radio plays the latest hits from America. We wait, a cool wind snapping at our jackets, hair in our faces.

Then the ferryman calls, and we start to descend the metal gangplank. Most of us settle in seats in the ship's lower hold. A few tourists climb high up on deck, with hats and scarves, bracing themselves against the wind.

When we arrive we will be in one place – here we are in another. The ferry's slow crawl; grey wake of the sea. In the distance, the island, hump-backed, crouches low, concealed in fog. Gannets, lit yellow with sun, drop needle-straight into the ocean.

Feet pad black air down the Scriggeen
road, laying a velvet trail beside my own.
A stoat trawls in and out of holes
in a stone wall. Lives between
the earth's core and the shores
of four thousand years ago.
What does the stoat know of time?
Night is salt and the blood of earthworms
bruising on the rain-damp floor.
Sniffs the air, flashes down its dark hole,
where time is stunned asleep
beside a pile of bloodied feathers.
Dead languages of birds
leap out into the frozen night,
call the old call to earth's shadowed cell.
Night birds flicker through the passages
of old men's sleep. Nothing changes.
A goat's gold eye strips a hedge.
The ivy grows thick. Trees are lungs,
gills dripping rain, loneliness a fog
to see through, a rain-torn path.
A heron lifts its wings, rows
through blue-black sky. Slowly,
the dark earth turns.

Spindle-drift of sea thrift
pinned to limestone floor;

wind-scoured wind-raked
bent-backed hawthorn.

Fuchsia bells nod and toll,
frisson in the wych elm grove,

scrape of briars: burred fingers
brush a stone wall –

Irish eyebright clings
to bitter soil.

AT TEAMPALL BHEANÁIN

A small church stands on a high hill, the roof
caved in. Who hewed the stones or cleared

the rubble are long gone. On the western wall,
a window stares past grazing fields, seeing

then forgetting. Light weaves loose matting
across the floor. Here, the clean fine wind

and the rock dove's call. Where they copied
the songs of sparrows on vellum.

Watched the planets glow, and knew the world
was round, for it spoke to them through

spring's return. Slept every night, wind-
blasted in a stone cell, as rain lashed across

the skin door, and comets dropped like torches
from some great hand. Men who loved

the earth and its mists that hang, a veil,
over prisms of sunlight they knew as God.

OCTOBER

Murray is not at the jetty
today, that bruised tongue of rock
where the lonely men go.

He pulls steaks from the sea,
offers them, in case I decide
to be his wife –

    Today I'm alone. Pause,
    then strip off my clothes

so I'm one band of skin, unbroken
as the sand that lies its arm
beside the ocean's cheek –

    Walk straight in,
    scissoring the cold.

THE WILD GOAT

He stands atop the broken jaw
of the cliff's edge –

ancient, ragged god
of high places. In the village,

sweet water in troughs,
nannies hobbled in chains,
white skirts lifted
by the goatherd's whip.

He knows the smallness
of this island earth,
the spider's trek
across a sun-baked rock,

ears cocked to the sound
of flight and chase,

scrabble of heels
to higher ground.

His yellow eyes stare out –
sunlight shatters
on limestone.

Below, the ocean butts
against the cliff's chest.

CILL ÉINNE BEACH

Two priests were lost here,
buried alive, the thick mud
of low tide turned
to quicksand.

Over the dunes, dark sand
a wound, the sea drawn back,
bright sheet of water,

they passed through,
robes torn by wind, a warning –

   heedless, they sank,

prayer, a cry of hunger
even as the world
dissolved them.

Now lovers shelter here,
gather kisses in the hollows
of their throats –

on the cusp of wave
and field, their hair
like flames upon the grass.

NIAMH

You go down deep. Touch the white pelt of winter
ocean, stroke the sand that rolls like bear fur, white-edged

softness of loosed minerals. Hair from the shore, seaweed
bands cold mouths around your burnt and salted skin.

You swim every winter's day; the ocean calls your feet
to make their way to the violet mouth of foam

and periwinkles. You feel them, clipped and silvered
under the ocean's shell, for cold makes us immune to slights

and slivers. A sliced toe on beach glass blooms to anemones
beneath the ocean's skin, four months of slicing open winter's

white-capped belly, sliding in. Once I saw you swim, an otter
or a winter bear, and stopped myself, for why does woman

become some other animal when she enters winter water, hair
curly and gold-tipped with salt and frost? Niamh, you move

slowly, shoulders rounded, fleshy pink. If I painted you
another way, if I only said you lived alone, cuticles raw

with coal dust, I'd be forcing emptiness into your days that isn't
there – for the ocean's mouth, barbed with blue, and seagrass

moving soundlessly across your feet receive you: free of flesh
and time, swimming out to meet the waves as all sea creatures do.

There is nothing in my bones that does not know these hills. This is
what I say to myself, daily, as I wander through the grounds
of the hostel, putting bottles into the recycle bin, opening
the windows, hanging sheets out to dry. The hostel sits on a
hilltop, and the hilltop opens to the sky. Cow bells clang like
a hundred tin rattles, the swaying udders heavy with milk.
No heart is safe from the sunrise at five thirty, the sky glossed
and rose-petaled. I ride from the top of the world and down,
daily, on my rounds to the shops, where I buy bread and
meat and vegetables, where the women talk to each other of
people – *Tomas, Máirtín* – I'll never know, no matter how
long I stay. I ride back from town and stop my bike at the
bottom of the hill, then walk, straining against handlebars,
back up to the cabin beside the hostel where I sleep.

At night the cows bellow to one another across the hills. *Where
are you going?* they seem to say to each other. The collared
doves' call is like a ball of wool rolling softly away. Their voices
echo on updrafts of wind, the downbeat of rain. *Whoot whooo
woo.* I occupy myself with cooking, making tea, listening to
mice scuttling across the rooftop. There is dust in the cabin so
I sweep it out. The hostel is three hundred years old, and the
island's landlord once lived here. The islanders will not drive
up the long driveway – they leave me at the bottom of the hill
if I get a lift. *A curse on this place,* they say. I hang sheets, empty
the water bucket outside. The landlord did not leave his ghost
– I find no traces of his spirit in the damp halls. I wonder if,
after he left, his love of the place ate into him like a burr.

From the window of my cabin I can see the shattered high cross on the next hill, only a stem left by Cromwell's army, a mossy ragged stump. The cracked remains of a round tower, and a standing stone, lined up on the diagonal, climbing the hill's flank. At the top there is Teampall Bheanáin, smallest church in Europe, built on an off angle, windows facing north and south, rather than east and west. The sunlight never fully gets in, or out – it founders in a corner, in a pool of dank water. The roof is long gone. Evenings the cows climb the hill for grazing, and leave soft piles of dung all around the church. Vegetable, animal, mineral, stone to stone, the grassy hilltop lives on. I watch the sun nest between the church's twin gables. The moon glows in the sky long before the sun has set. The earth provides two kinds of light; a heart can be in many places. Birds in the trees launch their calls, the collared dove sings *Whoot-wooo* as I close the kitchen windows, hang fresh towels in the rank-smelling bathroom. If the earth is an island, I feel close to its centre, watching all the living things returning to their homes: village, hilltop, pasture, cottage, nest.

Village

────────────

TWO

Two walk at night along the sea road
to Cill Rónáin, to Watty's pub then
home to Cill Éinne, a few grey houses
scattered on the road. Always the rain's
fury as they weave home, blown sideways;
always his hand reaches for her, pulls her
to the shoulder when the headlights blur.

BLOW-INS

Who huddle in jumpers, hands tucked in sleeves,
raw wool ticking the wrists. Fridays the session

at Joe Mac's pub or Saturdays at Tigh Fitz, but never
in daylight. Who live at the top of the road, in a shed

some farmer converted – ran a cable from his basement,
pulled in a spare bed. The mouldy thatch and dirt-

black floor, the windows webbed with cracks. Who
come to see the moon, unclothed and feral, the necks

of wych elm not quite breaking in the storm. Who watch
the sky turn black at four and grow thin beneath wool blankets.

Spring, the wind blows the mind open; winter, snaps it
shut. No one will follow you here, no one will knock.

SWEATER SHOP

Come in, dripping. New girl
at the cash hardly gives me a glance.
Maureen on the phone, the new shipment
late, Joyce brewing tea in the staffroom.
Stone cold of the flagstone floors –
how the heat rises to rafters. Liam
stacks boxes and talks of school,
his arm, bruised by the master.
Dust climbs the edges of sleeves;
lanolin leaves its scent on wool,
the animal stain. A video loops
all day: how the women here carded
their wool, bleached it in basins.
Soaked in sheep's urine, the video
claims, though Joyce shoots me a look,
mouths *Human.* Tourists arrive by
the boatload at ten, sift through stacks
of traditional sweaters, sewn by machine.
Niamh turns up and unsettles a pile.
At noon, a woman walks in from Mainistir,
breathless, a bag of hand-knit socks
to sell, hairnet streaming rain.

ROOTS

We sit under the sound of drizzle, storefront window
    blank with steam,
as if the shop were closed.

I risk a question: What do you think of us coming here,
    searching for roots?

He snorts and laughs, then wipes his face of it.

We don't mind you asking about ancestors – though it can
    be a bore. What we mind is the fecker from Texas come in
    the door drawling *Ahhhm from Cowneee Dawnny-Gaaal* like
    he owns the bloody country.

I laugh, look down. Ask him if he wants a tea, I'm going up
    to get one.

Picture the stranger in a ten-gallon hat, the bulk of
    his shoulders filling the doorframe –
There are no homecomings. The old world shifts by
    increments, and turns away.

THE BODHRÁN PLAYER

The bodhrán is a belly
that he brushes with the knuckles
of a drumstick –

    threads the blood's rhythm,
    thrums the blood's river –

clutches the drum as shy men
do, dearer than he'd hold
a woman. Rocks in his chair,
caught in the amber glance
of glasses on tables,

listens for the piper to unlock
the gimp of the reel:

it scampers out between rocks
and he follows it,

stutters his answer
low to the ground, where
the shrew dives down its hole –

    reels off, spitting words
we can't follow, chased
by the tapping of heels.

Then he hands me the drum
like a question –

   I run the bones
over tight goat's skin:

smell of dry grass
loosened by water, on

through the ring
of smoke and sweat, faces

fade and reappear, until

rhythm is a small wild
creature in my hands,
stroking the dark
cheek of the world.

WILD BIRD'S SONG

After the folk song "Es saß ein klein wild Vögelein"

Matthias sits with his guitar,
tuning strings back
to the Schwarzwald;

under the canopy,
boughs that bend heavy,
finds the song left
by his ancestors.

   Once,
a wild bird sat on a branch,
sang for herself alone.
A rich man, wrapped
in his thick fur cloak
offered silk and gold
if she would sing
for his pleasure.

The young bird flew
to the farthest field, sang
through the winter's night –
until hoar-frost bound her,
foot and wing.

There, if you look,
lying bleached among stones
are the bones of farmers' daughters,
fled from their villages.

Fathers would not look –
they took the parcels,
silken shirts and hair combs
tied with string,

stamped their anger
into the ground,
planted root vegetables
far down, where winter
could not touch them.

    So sing
  for those who lay down
  with their masters, sing
  for those who flew –
  who rest beyond
  the steepled towns

and sing for no one.

VILLAGE LIFE

A scrabble of roosters bars the door to the post office.

In the phone box, wind stirs an eddy of leaves.

Touring vans idle outside gift shops.

Men lean cheeks on hands gone soft.

SEA LEGS

A woman visiting from Hungary had never been to sea.

She climbed aboard the ferry.
When the winds took hold, they pulled the prow up,
    then let it go.
The boat seemed to sink, only to be grasped and hauled
up again, then dropped.
In the lurch and dive, she stared out the window, gasping.

When they picked her up at the pier, she didn't speak.
Spent three days in bed, staring at the wall.
Her mind still rocking.
Taking the measure of what held her.

On the fourth day, the storm cleared.
She sat up in bed, and stepped ashore.

West

STORM BEACH

Megaclasts beached and scattered,
a rock crust torn from the cliff
like a thumbnail. What wind
broke the bridle of the waves,
sent them leaping, heaved
boulders big as blocks on shore
to lie in waste? A grave-rubble,
the upturned face of shattered
karst – culled from the island's
edge, and then tossed back.

CENTRE: EOCHAILL

Rise with the centre of the island,
its thorny-backed middle. Climb,
upwards from the main road, follow
the steep incline of a goat path. Here,
the land pillaged and pocked by hoof-
prints, shudder and thunder of goat
heels driven to ground. Follow

the sound through the drone and wheel
of crickets: summer is gone, far gone.
On every side a stone wall, briars
that burrow the flesh. Walk where there
is no map – for grykes that open in limestone,
for blackthorn, moss-rot, rain pools, birds
that wing off. For here is the centre:

briars that blossom with fruit and die,
the scat of the herd, the sting of the flesh,
the wind that hurries its salt trail out
to the cliffs, to the ocean's surge and rise.

GRAVE (LEABA DHIARMUDA AGUS GHRÁINNE)

The bed of Diarmuid and Gráinne:

a dolmen over the booming earth.
Two boulders side by side, a capstone on top.
A space you can crawl into, but don't.

Two lovers traipsed across Ireland, seeking
peace from a king they had wronged.
The old scarred heart craving retribution.

Every place claims its heroes –
in England, in France, King Arthur sleeps.

Here, the goatherds pass, the ticks crawl.
Nettles rise up to claim the field.
Diarmuid and Gráinne rest,
or something does.

BURIAL GROUND

In this island a multitude of holy men
resided, and innumerable saints unknown
to all except Almighty God are here interred.
Anon.

Briar twisted on a stone wall;
nettles pierce the last
shards of day.

Thrones of light, thrones in sun –
seats of priests softened
with moss, the bruised

king's chair hung with blackberries.

Bones of the dead –
a great king, dead goat,
flecked with the dust of seaweed.

A saint's hand, a snail's shell.

Stonecrop grows through clefts in rock,
the fuchsia bushes hung
with bloodied bells.

THE HUNTER'S PATH

Oil-dark road below my bicycle wheels,
I pass beneath his blue window,
taking the Pleiades with me
on this journey home:

   the seven sisters, turned to doves,
fall through black-winged sky,
cross oceans, islands, olive groves
while Orion trails behind them.

Always, the god comes to steal away
the innocent who tarries on the hunter's path.
At night, the landscapes blur to one topography
where the face of the god looms, to pull me
to his Hades, or his blue room.

   The youngest Pleiade stalled
mid-flight, one tail feather caught
in the gates of eternity. Her sisters
died with her amid the star belt –

   now seven points of light remind us
constant flight is difficult,
though picturesque.

Calling us to race the wind
they shiver, high up,
defying destiny with one tail feather.

At my gate, I stop, breathe sharp iron air.
The lights are out, doors locked.
Desire sears its nightly trail
among the fixed cold bodies,

while the hunter gleams in his darkness,
    far behind.

Mornings, a white sweep. Sand. Wind
above whitecaps brimming and seething.

(The guidebooks say the name means "church among
the sand dunes," but the church has long since disappeared.)

On the hilltop behind, a changing shed. One
flag atop the flagpole flies the symbol for *beach*.

(Flaherty filmed here in '32 and '33. The twin thatched
cottages built for the film can be seen on the west side.)

One morning in October, three young women came to bathe.
They stood like lamp posts in the freezing wind.

(The thatched cottages now living out their separate
lives: one a tourist's gift shop, one a B & B.)

An older couple walked by and spoke to the bathers
in German. One leaned in to reply.

(Left on the fork in the road on the west side
of the beach you come into Cill Mhuirbhigh village.)

When the older couple had passed, the bathers turned
to each other, dropped their clothes in the sand.

(The first house you come to in the village was initially
a Protestant Bible school. Later, a constabulary barracks.)

On the hilltop, a boy watched from beside the changing shed.
In the sea, the bathers, and beyond them, a ship's white sail.

(Behind the craft shops is a home, now derelict. This began
as a cottage, grew into a guest house, post office, and shop.)

Seagulls rise up like foam from the surf. Sometimes
a currach, left tied to the pier, dashes itself against the sand.

37

PRE-ELECTRIC

No electric lighting here until the 1970s.

What was done, November evenings,
was lit by gas and wick. Tallow's drip, a backdrop;
the lamps' hiss, rain parting grass.

What was said – if anything – was said in half-lit rooms.
Always, an eye to the window sought the moon's curve,
plumbed the far-reaching dark.

Some nights, the skies over the Atlantic livid with light –
a world, kindled from within – and below
the small fires, the turf smouldering.

I'LL NEVER KNOW (AFTER READING SYNGE)

A greeting with God and Mary sewn in

Six months waiting for news from America

Seven miles' walk to the Sunday mass

Cold wooden weight of a creel

Dip of an oar through a screen of fog

Ache at the cliffs where the men went over

The sun sets on a windy beach;
last chimes of rain
slip from winter's belt.

*

Sun in me, nerves
exposed to light,
a tingling:

new love grows,
unlikely this spring,
tangling everything.

*

My lips, locked
around the sound O:

O fruit tree, stocked
with apples,
still unbloomed,

O calm of morning,
sleep clogged
with the calls of roosters,

birdsong opening
in the trees.

*

The ocean, white-capped –
slim sharp teeth
on a new dog.

Wind drives winter
out to sea –
    returns,
carrying spring
on its back.

As storms trawl
the beach, sand
worn brittle by frost –

what fingers
rake and trace, nightly,
    your hair?

NIGHT'S WORK

The wind that rocked the roof all night woke me:
opening gates, gusting behind the shed, strewing
bric-à-brac of pebbles, bones. Cow voices,
low as thorns, scraping the window. This is sleep,
probed awake. Sunflowers shaking their fists,
their waterdance patterning walls. Poppies aglow
in the afterdawn. Storm is night's work; rest, the sun
filling the sky's bowl. The waves work less and less.
Small leaves the rain had battened down, unfold.

I have wound down a shrinking path
that shrugs off to the right, toward a dry
gully of marram grass and sand. In this pit,
old shirts and bottle caps, cans of beer, nights
thrown into summer's fire. Past this pit,
the earth caves open – water heaves the sand
away, carving passageways through land.
Here the ocean bleeds into a seal-grey sky:
bruised clouds float across currents of mist,
as if a fist has punched through ice, cold water
seeping in. This year, the island turns its face
away. Ash-dark sand churns back into the surf;
bladderwrack and dillisk lie strewn across
the beach, weeds I learned to name.

II

Another Winter's Child

ANOTHER WINTER'S CHILD

He forced me down
in a mud-soiled patch,
my screams caught
behind the stone walls
barring one field from another.
My body, taken:
clogged with silt,
blocked then broken open.
Feet splayed out,
ankles twisting, useless –
a torn linen dress,
bloomers of my mother's knitting.
Black boots in mud,
my hands, feeble claws.
Not a thing
I could do
to stop it.

*

Weeks pass, shift
from rain to darkness.
Father's face sprung with rage
home late from the pub,
mother a hushed mouse
curled among blankets.

I bend over the coal stove baking
bread in the kitchen –
small brothers cling
to my apron.

Milk curdles sick for me;
all I eat is a drop of porridge,
grow heavy,
and wait.

*

I hold three eggs in my hand,
steaming with the heat
of their mother. Still lives

that will never hatch,
food snatched from the mouths
of my mother and brothers
as my pockets fill with coins.

Money grows in me.
I turn a stone ear to Danny when he cries,
fix porridge to fill their stomachs.

My eggs are my life, buried
deep in the folds of my dress
as I walk early to market,
the ravens and magpies
stripping the fields.

The young ones asleep
on their mats of straw.

I wash their dungarees
in the steaming tub,
under the crease
of my belly.

*

Out in the fields
with autumn's cusp
ringing in like church bells,
voices from the village
carry like dead leaves,
gather in corners.

I see my hands,
splayed across the stone wall:

red hands,
rough with the hoe
and with washing,
flakes of soap
in the basin
mixed with manure
on trouser cuffs.

The setting sun is a bleached sceptre
slicing across fields
dead and razed
for November.

Samhain.
I stand on the edge of this field,
a corpse
with new life growing inside,
like the green shoot
that steals the heart
of the turnip
asleep
in the cellar.

*

I dream
of a woman
who is the ocean.

I taste her
in the salt mist
that fills my throat
at dawn,
her voice
harsh in the storm
that makes the cattle lie down,
listening.

I hear her rage
pouring down
among hawthorn,
uprooting
the spines of oaks.

Mornings she retreats,
leaving her murmur
through stovepipes.

As I root through dust of coal
I whisper to her,
between shovels:

take me

*

I break from dreaming,
thick with sweat.

A slip of moon
is waning in the sky.
It's the clouds that stay still,
the moon that flies
like a scythe
through dense thickets
of night growth, night moss,
hoary and black.

I rise from bed,
gather my satchel of clothing,
money from eggs,

cross the kitchen
where their sleeping breath
mingles
with dying embers.

I walk heavily over the fields,
my weight pitching
over fine
grass hair cracking:

witches' lace, the cairns
of frost broken
by the path
I am making
to the sea.

*

Before me,
the ocean.

Rotted planks
heave with the sadness of passing feet.

The waves are oiled black;
they smell of summers
thrown overboard,
ruined grasses mixing
with its swell.

At the port,
women gather; wind
tears hair from their faces.
Words pass like smoke
through parted lips:

I'll not forget ye, Sean
God bless
   be smart
I'll be waiting to hear news
   of ye

Faces burrow
in must-darkened jackets,
arms clutch parcels,
open and close
like crows' wings.

I walk the raw planks
to the ship's hard shoulder.

On the docks
the women hang trembling
then blow apart,
scatter down laneways.

As the ship groans
and draws away,
I see their foreheads,
bleached with worry
under a scrap
of moon.

*

High on deck
I am a mountain smothered in rags,
not yet a mother,
not quite a woman.
I keep to myself,
sip tea and broth.

The ocean shimmers, watches me
with her gleaming eye.

She parts white wings of foam;
they rush along the ship's side,
are left behind
then gathered back to her.

She clenches her fists,
searing me from inside.
Grey fog fills
the column of my throat
as I cry out.
The captain scowls,
the women rush
to bring water.

The ocean mounts my belly,
salt waves flood
my white cotton shift.
I cling to the knife-thin edge
of moon, and bear down:
spreading open
over the fields,
gashed by the spade and harrow,
spasms of waves.
The ocean rocks me,
her sweat in my hair,
bridling my neck with icy teeth.

I push, push again,
and the warm weight
slides out of me –
relief of cold sky.

They bring scissors
and cut this child from me.
She is dead, still as a sparrow
in the grass
after a storm.
I wrap her tight as an egg
and watch her fall
into the ocean:

Marguerite,
small daughter
given over.

*

The ship rocks clear
into a wooden harbour.
I am bleached, freckled,
hair loose and dry
as wisps of clover.

I step off the plank
into a city of moving carriages:

a thin girl, tossed
across the ocean,
straight as a stick.

III

The Vine

Cado bilàdje
Soun lengàdje,
Cade auserou
Sa cansou.

(To each village
its own language;
to every bird
its song.)
  Occitan saying

THE OFFERING

Spring throws spears of light
from the Pic de Ger.

In the sleeping village,
twenty houses, stony grey,
doorways guarded by wisteria.
Tongues of mauve
on red roofs, cracked
and blistered skin.

Through Cazarilh,
tall trees are pared to posts,
hanging Jesus bronzed
in the sun's glare.
He wakes each day,
alone on the road,
silver light on his face.

Shrines to Mary
lit by bridal impatiens
flower in the dusk
of stone altars.
Votives dip and gutter;
wings of fog
touch flame.

Then, an open field.
Sheep the colour of raw milk
graze on grass and sun –

but one, her hind legs
stained, shivers as the wind
enfolds the lamb behind:

torn from the blood-sack,
wet with birth,
a fist, clutched
over something secret,

swaying on the grass
for the first time.

THE WILD BOAR

Rooting down, star-nosed,
snuffling for grubs,
breasts wet
with the gelatine of milk,

she is a muted sow,
a warrior –
still dark animal,
cloven.

Her tusks, wild
as rosebushes,
plunge in, slicing –

then out from the current,
intact. Scent of blood,
wild yarrow in the air.

When he shoots her,
one thought,
clear as a pellet

in the centre of her mind
is a crashing
back to the scented herd,

charging slowly
through her own blood.

Now she hangs,
still furious, on the wall.
Monstrous in her beauty,

her eyes of glass
have forgotten the place
she was running to.

AUGUST, VALLÉE DE LA BAROUSSE

In the valley, vines
rise coiled from the earth,
the cries of Roman slaves
mixing with birdsong.

We stand shoulder to shoulder
with plague time
battling in like a raven –

shunting across towns,
sparing the highest villages,
leaving cracks and shudders
and wasting.

We lie pillow to head on stone
with illiterate travellers:

runners from Toulouse
with dreams of packages
and mandolins that play all night,

serving girls with eyes
dark as grapes,
and the salt kiss
of olives on a platter.

In the beat of a pheasant's wings
or a gentian opening at dawn:

a multitude of stories
layer upon layer,
pink saxifrage sneaking through.

In the charcoal smudge
of paint and clay,
burnt umber left on the brush
of the day along the roadside,
by farmers' fields razed
to the ground

we find the sole of a shoe,
remnant of centuries,
soft wood
made denser by rain.

The breath of a dandelion:
peasants' food, peasants' wine,

and the turrets of lords
and landowners
keeping watch over the valley.

The hills leave gaps in the night.
Beyond the village walls,
stacks of barks from dogs
break through, unexplained.

While we sleep, the sound
of shepherds' feet
moving over the hills,
searching for lost lambs
or patches of dung
to throw into their fires,

until darkness retreats
down the mountainside, pierced

by the needle-voices of birds.

THE VINE

The hour shone gold. Long, it divided evening
from day. I stepped out, hair in a braid, feet
cracking the copper dust of the road. Past houses
with combs of wisteria, shuttered, faces turned
inward. In backyards, a thin black dog with
a white face, men playing *boules*, boys
shouting in packs while mothers combed the air
with their voices. I walked out past the houses,

into the vineyards. Slipped in between rows,
where roots sank into the soil – reaching down
where the breath of aqueducts lingers, breath
and the sound of sandals on soil, the heat
of the hands that lifted the vines, and the grapes
crushed into urns. I wove deeper, breaking
dry ground again, drunk on the smell of the grapes,
wild and fine, the dregs of day tossed over my shoulder.

LES CAGOTS

No one knows ... why the cagots were ostracized and persecuted ...
In the South-west, it was largely believed that their ancestors
were Visigoths defeated by King Clovis in the sixth century. Their name
was said to derive from the Bearnese or Latin for "Goth dog," though
it was more likely to be related to a word for excrement.
Graham Robb, *The Discovery of France: A Historical Geography*, 2007

In the mountains
   (the woman, Marie-Pierre,
     her little house near Tarbes)

   the history,
     obscure
   traced
     through villages

carpenters, basket-makers
   (the wrong parts of town)
   marked
     for a thousand years

an inferior caste
  Agotes, Gahets

the people   divided
  Capets, Caqueux

in districts
      the malarial   side of the river
known as
      Cagoteries

in Campan
  in Hagetmau

in churches   their own
    doors, own
        fonts

communion
     on the end
of a wooden spoon

(report
    their presence
by shaking a rattle)

hewers
of wood
    drawers
    of water
  made

    barrels
    for wine
coffins
for the dead

  built
    churches
    from which they were

        excluded

forbidden
  to walk barefoot

  (gave rise to the legend
    of webbed toes)

to touch the parapets
  of bridges

  a goose's foot
    pinned
    to their clothes

caught using the font:

   a hand
      nailed
      to the church door

who farms
his fields:

      feet pierced
      with iron

their humble cemeteries
    in Bentayou-Sérée

      north of Pau

short, dark, and stocky
   (or blond and blue-eyed)
scattered across

   Gascony
      Navarre

lepers
   or slaves
of the Goths or
      Saracens
   or
skilled woodworkers

      (rivalry regimented over time)

the pestiferous people

in Campan
   you can still see

(her daughter Sylvie, the darkest
   in her class)

   (if people knew)

IV

The Silken Threads

THE SILKEN THREADS

Economic antagonisms exist in nearly every labor movement,
yet something else happens that sets the movement in motion.
In Lyon, it was the working conditions ... Air was not circulated,
as windows were vehemently prohibited from being opened ...
There were even tunnels leading from building to building so that
the silk would never be exposed to the outside air during manufacturing.
Erika Budde, "Silk in Lyons," Northampton Silk Project

There is a beating of wings
when you shift in the sheets –
moth's breath rustles the curtains.
In the front room, the loom waits,
lewd giant, hungry for your fingers,
the lean of your shoulder
over the grain of the cloth.
The warp and weft
unbroken, your eyes locked
in secret patterns
of paisley, damask,
as a griffin floats across the screen.
Braiding and unbraiding
the silken threads
your eyes are glossed as wet stones,
bluer than dye.

Dawn spills, russet
as the blood of weavers.
Soon you will stir, rise,
one thin stem of wheat
among a field of others.
Across Croix-Rousse
all wake in narrow rooms, swaying:
cough the rattle-cough,
the lungs' pulleys dipped in ash,
coated with the raw dust
of the cloth. You move
to the washbasin, soap skin
the colour of wax,
sip strong tea and begin
the tapping of the loom.

It spins and cords the muscles
tight across your back,
your arms as heavy
as wet branches.

Hours blend
as strings of sunlight
scale the window.
When the room is dark
you stumble into bed;
only our words of loving
still the sound of the loom

before the great silk curtain
of sleep lowers you
with vermilion, russet and gold
to that dim place,
the island in the sea
of exhaustion.

*

Our son,
fourteen years old and gone.
Silk loom gnarled his hands.
Hands that have loved no woman
but know the cloth
like the lover's nape
caught midstream in a bath
and slipping under
soft-petalled water –

His gelid stare as he left,
one who walks
with no destination,
trained from birth
for the trade

as the tree
bent under brutal winds
knows only to grow
one way.

*

The streets are ropes of jute
thick with mud.
In the rugged district
weavers shiver
outside dormitories.
In the slats of sunlight
stolen between shifts,
men smoke on doorsteps,
stoke their anger.

A second storm
is brewing over Croix-Rousse,
they say.
Some squint and glance up the street,
remember themselves
with raised fists
and the National Guard
in clothing red and blazing.

Women rub tired hands
over yellow eyes.
When we strike again,
let them come.
More fire for the furnace of hatred
that broils, this season.

In airless rooms
the colours spin on.
Merchants from Versailles command them
from the bent-backed child's fingers,
a small figure braiding
yellows that set the sallow walls alight.
Rose tendrils climb
the trellis of the loom
as an old man
bleeds into a brocade
for some clergyman's sitting-room in Vienna –

In the Saône, the dyes run green
as if new gods
have spilled their blood,
and blue, from the tears of fishes –

*

Monsieur Michel takes the bundle
from my hands
and pays us his pittance.
The merchant's eyes, round as black *sous*
take in the redness of my hands,
the darkness of the room,
the slow fire of the loom
burning our thoughts
to crimson ends.

Our children
learn the spectrum's slide
from red to mauve
before they know words.
We pluck patterns like birds
from the air
and fasten them with strings.
Beneath the city's
damp belly we tunnel,
sheltering our bright burdens
from the teeth of rain,
the bleaching sun.

Silk has the look of skin.
It is a live thing,
stolen threads that remember
a living worm
in its dying chamber,
a loose-fitting cloak
passed from moths to kings.
It has the curves of a body,
the weight of a sleeping child.

It passes like water
out of our hands.

*

A riot of leaves
blows across the courtyard,
wind's fingers
brush the backs of our hands
while we wait in this stillness.

Across the city
the looms are abandoned
like dishes after a banquet
of blood and dye.
The young men stream
like mice from the darkness,
soon to erupt
in the streets.

In the Vieille Ville,
horses' hooves dance metallic
over cobblestones,
silver-bitten grey
gleaming church steps.

The sandstone face
of St Jean's Cathedral,
burnt clay of a doorway,
a shopkeeper on Rue Juiverie
keeping time with his broom.
The tinkling bells of a door open:
brown shoes scuffle in,
silver coins are exchanged
for a loaf of bread, a sack of flour.
A flea-bitten dog outside St Paul's
battles flies with his grey ears.

These are the colours of the day.
We drink them heavily
like sweet brown tea
these few hours
before the marshals
and the blockades
and the shrieking colours
that beg to be woven.

There are spaces we make for ourselves
between shadow and sunlight,
rare threads pulled
from the skein of darkness.

When your fingers sift
through the loose strands
of my hair
and clothing falls from us
like dead sheaves, revealing
the living fibre of the skin,
I know this is the light
we must choose to live by.

Even the night enfolds our bodies
in its finest silken sheets.

V

The Burning House

ROSE

in memory of Rose Devlin

Awake at night with the roaches, hearing
their scramble, tumble of their lives;
upstairs and down, the shake and scuttle
of other people's children.

Your lover creeps up the back stairs,
numb from wherever his day has taken him.
You're never sure – only know the weight
of his steps across the tile floor,
smell of his breath past dinnertime.
It is only the two of you; his children
scattered between mother and aunts.
Your own are with their father,

Nonnie's hair falling out of braids
like wet silk, greasy if she forgets to wash it.
The boys pitching stones behind the shed –

Your husband comes home, to the house
that you left. He bangs cupboards, searching
for pots and pans, boils a simple meal
for himself and Nonnie, if she'll eat.

Her grades are good this year, despite
three sore throats that lasted weeks.
You came home for her fever,
one afternoon when he was working.
The curtains were thin; light filtered through.
She lay on the couch under a blanket.
You leaned over her face, wished for a moment
that she wouldn't remember you,
only a distant scent, the smell of mother.
She is seven, remembers everything.

You leave, but also stay behind
in that house, looking out to the back alleys,
the laundry on clotheslines in rows.
You watch the sun set over the tops of buildings.
Then his foot in the door and you disappear,
small as the rain that gathers in gutters and pipes.

   Once
you walked to the Royal Mountain in spring.
You were a girl in a blue dress; the nuns
had let you out early, and you ran from the convent walls
to the hills that are covered in sun.
You wanted to see a show, but the men in theatres
touched you, strange men with fat fingers and stale smells.
They reminded you of fathers – they could be
your own; he is gone, like a grain of sun.
The sunlight moves over your piece of grass,
and you follow it. Shadow-spots grow wider
and colder if you stay too long.

Tripping, choir songs in your head,
you open the door and wait for Mother,
lock it, and hear the silence after it closes
except for the old clock that somebody else bought.
None of this furniture belongs to Mother,
though she says it does. You know these rooms
do not belong to you, as surely as
your time at school does not exist:

after the bell rings, you skip and scatter,
and who knows where anybody ends up, then?
One could end up anywhere, Mother
could have chosen these rooms, or the ones
up the street, it would have been the same.

You sit and wait, watch the light playing.
Outside was a fine day.

FOR ÉMILE NELLIGAN

On Laval Street, leaves rise twisted
in the wind's snare
and building facades shiver –

night has a shaded face,
a cry pressed into
frozen vines.

On the balcony
did you sit, thought-heavy,
high up from the wave-rocked

street, sure of the poems
that were your life, a breakwater,
tides reaching far from here?

This city that you left
has lightened from grey.
Summer in the park

past six o'clock,
the drummers dressed
in sweat and rain –

Still, I know your face
from the photograph.
In your eyes we see

the bite and hammer
of winter's true hand.
I cannot go with you,

forty years into silence,
but shall stand on the edge
of a cracked

sidewalk for a moment
in your city
and say to you,

This is where the shades
of light and colour are
about to fall.

THE BURNING HOUSE

I knew what I had and what I stood to lose.
I held it cradled in my arms, eyes open even as I slept.
                                        Paul Monette

Dying men fall upon the grasses this year.

Evenings I walk
pulled by the wind tunnel of the long streets,
river of sky.

I come upon bodies, lying in ditches –
we know each other
as leaves pressed together after rain.

I stop and weep for their cold eyes,
hands like lilies
half closed

in the blue snaking light
of the blue season.

Stories have no rest –

  books with pulses, letters
    etched
into the skin of my stomach.

Wind blows through this room
their hands, leaves
that touch to my window.

In the rooms of lovers,
bodies curl into each other
trembling in heat.

A pod of milkweed sprung open by wind:

    one will leave the house of his body
    as the other tries to hold him back.

All that is full is the bed.

While fever rages hoarse outside the door
I am listening to their voices through the trees.

Roger,

I stormed the streets after you left, Paris
with her cancer face. The wind roars up alleys –
pieces of music trail out of doorways. Women in parlours
   cough
when violet evening hits the window.

I lay in the grass. There was no morning.
A shell in my ear heard the waking of molluscs, groans
from the bottom of some dead sea.

By the monuments of Greece, with the sun-chain wrapping
   around us –

We looked into the eyes of the sun at Knossos. Saw none
   of this.

                                                        Paul

Hoarse with listening

I push the window up, let the night in.
Touch my skin where you have been and gone.

When the fever waltzes in
it leaves your fingermarks upon my body.

You shudder three times before sleeping
bones wired with a cold I can't feel.

Can I not drift with you

can't we find a gentle river

can't I turn over
in the warm mud and be with you?

All that is full is this bed.

I cup your face in my hands
sleeping so still and delicate as water.

Paul,

Evenings by the window, the garden shot with gold –
in its hole, the eye glazes over.

The hour when the bats fly, low at twilight, your hand on
   my cheek,
fingers dialling messages to me –

Keep the garden at the centre of your eye, dahlias
a hot sun. Remember
the shadows of birds, where they fell.

I tell you

   a river runs pain through my eyes
   the garden flying in pieces
   cold on my cheek
   the minute your fingers leave me

   when once, you closed the river with your hands.

                                        Roger

On the trail with you
hand in your hand

spray of dusk
through a halo of trees

weak knees, your fingers
pressed into my hand, bones

fingers of shadow
brush over
the body of night

it moves through the forest
finds a dark corner
to rest –

we lie, spread open
on the earth

trees bent low
night on our faces.

Do you remember
   the smell of my hair in rain?

We started on a park bench
later on, at my house

I sang to you
though my voice
was a burr through the smoke.

Now you're
the moon,
  half full.

I walk every night
through the chill –

  your garden

thrown and wary

  a husk in winter sun.

Rog,

What will happen
to the garden on King's Road
after you're gone?

The sun will make
a lousy gardener
plans torn up by wind

autumn a foul breath
me in the quiet living room
everything in pantomime

clothes on the line
will not dry now
hard grey dust
where we cleaned

I'll tell you something
the neighbours don't know

this is a burning house –
water pipes bursting
sounds from within
like screaming

a family of two men
trying to get outside –

Paul

Summer, violets in the air

I walk home at midnight
past the street where we lived

wind like water
lapping the sidewalks

no bottom, no shore
night is a river

carries me deep
away from your body

I walk home
through water.

Love rises in the trees,
palpable.

I see it
through the back door:

a storm
has turned the trees
to ice cages,
their leaves,
savage fruit.

Shadows of birds
skim the edges
of the garden.

When they will leave
I cannot say

   where they shall fall

   how long they might stay.

I carried you through Paris.

We drifted through puddles
violet night
poured over us, the grey city
turned up her hands

your palms burned up, eaten right through
yellow water on the brow

I was looking for a pillow or a church
some place where I could lay you down
concrete steps or a half-opened doorway

your body floated in my arms, head on my chest
a skull, still your eyes smiling out of it

violets and blue air and palms eaten up

the streets were a poison
on every corner a man would sell us
what fragments he could pull from his pocket
fingers, toes, a loose tooth, soft elastic lips –

boys like willow sticks
lined the alleys when the shops closed down

I carried you in the twilight filled with streetlamps

a boy was planted dead still
in the centre of the street, palms floating open
white lilies hanging in the near dark.

I laid you on a bench.

The river shone slick as oil, pulling the night in.

IN AZÉ (ARS POETICA)

Once, in Azé, I left the crowded school
and found a road leading into the vineyards.
Strode into an opening between rows. Here
the vines grew high above my head, thick
as ropes. I walked among them. Dust settled
and the sky grew dark. Rain began; the earth
blackened. Caught as though among a crowd,
I looked down. The edge of a white stone pillar
stuck through the earth, bare as a shoulder bone.
I knelt and touched what the rain had freed:
a pattern of birds and leaves. Partridges, vines.
Terra cotta, sky-washed teal. Under my feet
lay a villa, a village of stone. I wanted to
call for someone, but the vines only carried
my voice so far and the rain's voice was louder.
So I stayed, hunkered down, tracing bird-tipped
patterns with my fingers, clearing mud to read
the flower-script that springs up, parts the soil.

NOTES

CILL MHUIRBHIGH BEACH

The text in parentheses is adapted from page 67 of *Legends in the Landscape: A Pocket Guide to Árainn,* by Dara Ó Maoildhia. "Flaherty" refers to American filmmaker Robert J. Flaherty, who directed the 1934 film *Man of Aran,* a fictional documentary about life on the Aran Islands.

I'LL NEVER KNOW (AFTER READING SYNGE)

The Irish author and playwright John M. Synge made several trips to the Aran Islands between 1898 and 1902. In 1907, he published *The Aran Islands,* an account of his time on Inis Mór and Inis Meáin.

NIGHT'S WORK

"The waves work less and less" is borrowed from "Alas! so all things now do hold their peace!" by Henry Howard, Earl of Surrey. This poem was inspired by a writing workshop taught by Mary di Michele and Susan Gillis.

LES CAGOTS

The text in this poem was culled and rearranged from the article "The Last Untouchable in Europe," published in the *Independent* by Sean Thomas in 2008.

Émile Nelligan was a French-Canadian poet, born in Montreal in 1879. He wrote most of his poems between the ages of sixteen and nineteen. He was hospitalized in 1899 after exhibiting signs of mental illness, and remained in hospital until his death in 1941.

THE BURNING HOUSE

The American writer Paul Monette wrote *Borrowed Time: An AIDS Memoir*, which chronicles the last nineteen months of his life with long-time partner Roger Horwitz, before Horwitz died of AIDS. Paul Monette died of AIDS complications in 1995. The epigraph is drawn from *Borrowed Time: An AIDS Memoir*.

ACKNOWLEDGMENTS

Thanks, first of all, to my immediate and extended family. This book could not have been written without the love, dedication, and support of my mother, Norah Maynard. I am grateful to my father, Fred Drukker, annotator of manuscripts, for his unflagging encouragement. Thanks to my brothers Jesse, Jeff, and Bruce, my nephew Christopher, and my uncle Eddy Maynard and family for cheering me on. My uncle Bob Maynard's generosity and presence are a blessing. My grandparents Bridey Mary Rose Devlin, Robert Maynard, Alida Koymans, and Sydney Drukker enriched my life with their stories, and are never far from my mind. Thanks to Michael Carruthers for his support. Thanks to Norah Maynard and Michael Carruthers, Bob Maynard, Dinah Daigneault, and Gillian Crouse for opening their homes to me and offering me places to write over the years. Thanks to the community of Morin Heights for providing a solid home base and peaceful walking trails.

Thanks to Benjamin Lefebvre for his friendship and support, and for practical help of all kinds. Thanks to Sandy Pool, Lisa Richter, Norah Maynard, Fred Drukker, Jacob Letkemann, James Buchanan, Gillian Crouse, Meredith Darling, Rolf Brabander, Susan Steudel, Gabrielle McIntire, Caroline Clark, Chloe Collins, the cohort of the 2010 Banff Writing Studio, the cohort of the 2009 Sage Hill Writing Experience, and my colleagues in the English department at Concordia for reading many different versions of these poems, for helpful comments, and for keeping me company on the journey. Thanks to Ilona Martonfi, John Fretz, and Hugh Hazelton for their frequent invitations to read in Montreal. Ian Ferrier and Carolyne Van der Meer offered generous feedback during the editing stages.

Thanks to Nonie O'Neill on Inis Mór for her friendship and hospitality, and for answering so many of my questions about the flora and fauna of the Aran Islands. Thanks to Cheryl Murphy and family in Ballina, and Denise Heneghan and family in Galway for welcoming me into their homes. I am grateful to Dara Molloy, Tess Harper, and their children for their hospitality at An Charraig, and to Emese, Karen, Simon, Alle, Matthias, Maja, and Daniel for music, laughter, and community when I lived on Inis Mór. Thanks to Irmtraud Mair, Helmut Reubelt, and Benny McCabe for entrusting me with the care of a beautiful stone house in Iar Áirne, where several of these poems were written.

Thanks to Jacqueline Peyrot for taking me under her wing during my time in the Pyrenees, and for teaching me about *les cagots* and their history. Thanks to Maité Vermeil and family for warmth and accommodation in Arcizans-Avant. Thanks to Dana Colette, travel companion extraordinaire.

My deepest thanks to Carolyn Smart at McGill-Queen's for editing this collection, and for her listening ear, patience, and attention to detail. Many thanks to Mark Abley and Allan Hepburn at McGill-Queen's for reading and helpful comments, and to Kathleen Fraser for treating the manuscript with such care. Special thanks to Stephanie Bolster for her support and friendship, and for helping me to shape so many of the poems in this collection. Karen Connelly's mentorship, spark, and insight guided me through the early stages of writing. I am grateful to John Barton, Susan Cahill, Mary di Michele, Gary Geddes, John Glenday, Don McKay, Siobhán Ní Mhaolagáin, Gearóid Ó hAllmhuráin, Norman Ravvin, and Anne Simpson for generous feedback. Thanks to Bill Jones for early encouragement. Thanks to the late Ruth Taylor, mentor and teacher.

Many thanks to the *Malahat Review*, *Contemporary Verse 2*, *The Montreal International Poetry Prize Longlist Anthology*, *Room* magazine, *enRoute* magazine, the *SHOp*, the *Island Review*, *Literary Review of Canada*, *carte blanche*, and *Headlight Anthology* for publishing some of the poems in this collection, in both their present and earlier forms. Thanks to C B C Radio for airing an abridged version of "The Silken Threads" read by actress Donna Carroll White on *Between the Covers*, and for airing my reading of "Night on the Dark Earth" on *Cinque à Six*.

I am very grateful to the Canada Council for the Arts, the Conseil des arts et des lettres du Québec, the English Department and School of Canadian Irish Studies at Concordia University, the Banff Centre, Sage Hill, the Humber School for Writers, the CBC Literary Awards, CBC Radio, and *enRoute Magazine* for their support and encouragement.